Coming Home

Advent/Christmas Sermons
From The Book Of Haggai

Frank Ramirez

CSS Publishing Company, Inc., Lima, Ohio

COMING HOME

Scripture quotations are from the *New Revised Standard Version of the Bible*, copyright 1989 by the Division of Christian Education of the National Council of the Churches of Christ in the USA. Used by permission.

Library of Congress Cataloging-in-Publication Data

Ramirez, Frank, 1954-
    Coming home : Advent/Christmas sermons from the book of Haggai / Frank Ramirez.
        p.   cm.
    ISBN 0-7880-1281-9 (alk. paper)
    1. Bible. O. T. Haggai—Sermons. 2. Sermons, American. 3. Advent sermons. 4. Christmas sermons.   I. Title.
BS1655.4.R35   1998
252'.61—dc21   98-9764
                                                                                                    CIP

This book is available in the following formats, listed by ISBN:
    0-7880-1281-9   Book
    0-7880-1282-7   IBM
    0-7880-1283-5   MAC
    0-7880-1284-3   Sermon Prep

PRINTED IN U.S.A.

To Ellen Daniels,
who loves to read almost as much
as she loves the Lord

Table Of Contents

Introduction

Some people call it hackwork. Writing to a formula. Well, if so, Shakespeare was the greatest hack writer who ever lived. He wrote 154 sonnets, fourteen lines of iambic pentameter, rhymed *abab cdcd efef gg*, adhering to the same form but springing forth surprises with every poem.

I've got friends who are romance writers, and they write novel after novel, adhering to the same form and breathing new life into their subject matter with every new book. I admire the ability to stick to a form and make it work.

As a preacher I do the same myself. Twenty minutes a Sunday, covering a lot of the same ground every three years with the lectionary. It's a challenge and I enjoy it. Preaching is probably my favorite task of the ministry.

But after fifteen years of the first three chapters of Luke and the first two chapters of Matthew, I decided I wanted to preach about something a little different around Christmastime. I'd been doing some reading about the prophet Haggai, and it occurred to me there were some Christmas sermons inside that tiny book.

After writing the sermons I turned to this little study. My hobby is freelance writing, and I know that written English and spoken English are two different languages. Producing this study involved rewriting the sermons from scratch, and including a lot of material I could squeeze into the spoken messages.

All scripture is taken from the *New Revised Standard Version of the Bible*. All quotations are from the book of Haggai unless otherwise indicated.

In addition to various study Bibles, I relied upon the June, July, August 1991 issue of *A Guide For Biblical Studies* written by Chris Bucher; "Micah-Malachi" by Ralph L. Smith; Volume 32 of the

Word Biblical Commentary by Carol L. Meyers and Eric M. Meyers; "Haggai, Zechariah 1-8" by Carol L. Meyers and Eric M. Meyers from *The Anchor Bible*; and *The International Theological Commentary* "Haggai and Zechariah: Rebuilding With Hope" by Carroll Stuhmueller, C.P.

I find the minor prophets very attractive. Each is a world unto itself, anchored to a particular place and time, yet because of the action of God's spirit, the whole of the gospel is contained in each book.

> The Lord bless you and keep you. I remain
> Christ's servant and yours,
> Frank Ramirez

The Word Of The Lord
Came To The Prophet Haggai

In the second year of King Darius, in the sixth month, on the first day of the month, the word of the LORD came by the prophet Haggai to Zerubbabel son of Shealtiel, governor of Judah, and to Joshua son of Jehozadak, the high priest....
                                                            — Haggai 1:1

Now the prophets, Haggai and Zechariah son of Iddo, prophesied to the Jews who were in Judah and Jerusalem, in the name of the God of Israel who was over them. Then Zerubbabel son of Shealtiel and Jeshua son of Jozadak set out to rebuild the house of God in Jerusalem; and with them were the prophets of God, helping them.
                                                            — Ezra 5:1-2

There is something about seeing a zero creep up on the odometer, whether it's in your car, the world, or your life, that makes you take notice. Yes, it's just a mathematical accident. The zero wasn't even invented until around a thousand years ago, and we just happen to use base ten, which makes numbers like 10, 100, and 1,000 seem significant,

Still, the zero is a handy marker. There is nothing like watching 100,000 roll over on a car's odometer. Each birthday that ended in 0 (10, 20, 30, and 40) has seemed significant to me. And of course, the end of a decade always seems like a good time to take stock of the most recent chunk of history.

Sometimes we jump the gun. I remember *Life* magazine published a retrospective of the '80s with about four months to go in

1989. It seemed like a safe thing to do. The big events had already occurred, and surely nothing that significant could happen in the remaining days.

Except, of course, that the waning hours of the decade saw the fall of communism in Eastern Europe, the collapse of the Iron Curtain and the Berlin Wall, and the planting of seeds that led to the dissolution of the Soviet Union. Fairly significant stuff, I'd say.

As a matter of fact, some people called it the end of history. No longer would the world be divided into two ideological camps, east and west, free world and communist. The day of jubilee had arrived! It was a time of rejoicing.

And there was every reason to rejoice, because to a great extent the danger of MAD (Mutually Assured Destruction) had passed. There was talk that a lot of the money spent on armaments would be turned into a peace dividend, as swords were bent into plowshares. We'd all be singing in the sunshine.

But the world didn't stop. Nation still took up sword against nation. The Armenians and the Azerbaijanis took up arms against each other. Iraq swallowed Kuwait and was made to spit it out. North Korea took everyone to the brink. India and Pakistan played nuclear chicken. And we haven't even brought up the mess in the former Yugoslavia!

History didn't stop, but it changed. There were still pressing demands. And a lot of important things we hoped we'd take care of had to be put on hold. How long, we wondered, would we have to wait until we could take care of the widows and orphans?

The book of Haggai was written after the end of history as well. God's people had been in exile for as long a time as the Communist empire lasted — about the length of a human life. As a matter of fact, that's one of the delicious ironies of the book of Daniel. The young Daniel introduced in the first chapter outlives the Babylonian empire which carried him off.

The exile began in bitterness, expressed best in Psalm 137:

> *By the rivers of Babylon — there we sat down and there*
> *we wept when we remembered Zion.*

10

On the willows there we hung up our harps.
For there our captors asked us for songs, and our tor-
mentors asked for mirth, saying, "Sing us one of the
songs of Zion!"
How could we sing the Lord's song in a foreign land?
If I forget you, O Jerusalem, let my right hand wither!
Let my tongue cling to the roof of my mouth, if I do not
remember you, if I do not set Jerusalem above my
highest joy.

Conversely, there was overwhelming joy when the exiles returned! As was written in Psalm 126:

When the LORD restored the fortunes of Zion, we were
like those who dream.
Then our mouth was filled with laughter, and our tongue
with shouts of joy; then it was said among the na-
tions, "The LORD has done great things for them."
The LORD has done great things for us, and we rejoiced.
Restore our fortunes, O LORD, like the watercourses in
the Negeb.
May those who sow in tears reap with shouts of joy.
Those who go out weeping, bearing the seed for sowing,
shall come home with shouts of joy, carrying their
sheaves.

There were big plans for the new Israel. It wasn't going to be
quite the same, but after waiting three generations to return, the
survivors could hardly wait to get started.

Only they couldn"t get started. Here's the chronology. The
Temple of Jerusalem was destroyed around the year 586 B.C. The
Babylonian Empire, like others before it, deported conquered
peoples, moving them across the map like chess pieces. This was
supposed to lead to a loss of identity. Instead, with God's help,
Israel's sense of destiny was strengthened. God's people gained a
stronger self-identification.

In 539 Cyrus the Persian conquered Babylon, and a year later
the first exiles returned. His Persian Empire attempted something
rather grand. It returned nations to their lands, and encouraged the

11

practice of their local religion. The idea was that these regions, autonomous in some things while recognizing the overarching authority of the Emperor, would be loyal and cooperative.

The Eber Nahara, the larger province of Beyond the River, contained the subprovince of Yehud, the Aramaic word for Judah. This is where the Temple would be rebuilt. It was supposed to be the start of a new golden age. God's people would meet in the restored Temple to glorify his name.

Nothing much came of the attempt to rebuild the Temple. Oh, it began. So we read in Ezra's history:

> *When the builders laid the foundation of the temple of the LORD, the priests in their vestments were stationed to praise the LORD with trumpets, and the Levites, the sons of Asaph, with cymbals, according to the directions of King David of Israel; and they sang responsively, praising and giving thanks to the LORD, "For he is good, for his steadfast love endures forever toward Israel." And all the people responded with a great shout when they praised the LORD, because the foundation of the house of the LORD was laid. But many of the priests and Levites and heads of families, old people who had seen the first house on its foundations, wept with a loud voice when they saw this house, though many shouted aloud for joy...."*
> — Ezra 3:10-12

But there were problems. The returnees thought they were hot stuff, while those that had remained behind, the landless and impoverished, thought they were the true remnant. These latter came to be known as the Samaritans. You would think the two sundered branches of the family would greet each other with joy, but there's nothing like cousins for feuding. A lot of energy was expended in the struggle. A few bribes were made by Judah's enemies. Suddenly there were difficulties with the building permits.

The ones called "the people of the land," those who had remained behind during the exile, filled the people of Judea with fright. These distractions may have fueled the discouragment of the people, but underneath it all may have been a lack of will to complete the project from the beginning.

The temple project ran out of steam. This sounds surprising, but not when you consider it.

I remember when my wife and I traveled to Scotland in 1987. A cabby drove us up a hill overlooking Edinburgh to show us a spot called by two different names: The Scots National Monument, and the Scottish National Shame.

What the traveler finds are three sides of a monument patterned after the Parthenon of ancient Athens. It was intended to house a museum celebrating the Scots' national spirit. The pillars are there, but the money ran out, and no one would take responsibility for the project. The longer it languished, the more difficult it was to resume the project. No one would take responsibility. Soon it became a local joke. The pillars are still there, but the temple to the Scottish spirit remains unfinished.

I find the longer you put off an important job, the harder it is to resume it later. A few years ago our fellowship decided to order signs that directed people to our country church. The task itself was not a big one, but there were always more pressing day-to-day duties for the trustees to take care of: leaky roofs, flooded basements, broken fences, stubborn boilers. The signs were finally made after some months, and then languished while others looked into the local codes regarding the placement of signs. The actual labor involved was minimal, but it took over three years for the signs to make their appearance.

And then there was the parsonage basement. One year I worked out a deal where I would forego a raise for a year if the church would build a new bedroom in the basement. Everyone was in favor of it. As the months slipped by, everyone in the church agreed that the room should be built, would be built; but nothing was done.

Others might have worried, but I knew that at some point a prophet would appear. The Lord would commission someone, speaking to them in their heart, to get the job done. After all, it wasn't a big job. It wasn't going to take years. Just a short period of leadership was needed for the task to be accomplished.

13

Enter the newly elected chair of trustees. He hadn't actually built a room before, but he'd helped here and there, worked at a lumber yard, and was handy with a hammer. No sweat. It was already mid-October, but he decided he'd marshal the troops and get that room done.

All it took was a leader. The materials and workers were there, just waiting. And it wasn't a long job either. A few Saturdays, a handful of weeknights, spread over the course of a few weeks, and it was done. New bedroom.

That's what Haggai was. A prophet in season.

Meanwhile, the outside world continued. In the year 522 the emperor Darius ascended to the throne of the Persian empire. Over the next two years he consolidated his empire, appointed Zerubbabel governor of Judea, and gave permission for work to start again on the Temple.

Enter the prophet Haggai. On August 29 of 520 Haggai first spoke to the people. His last recorded utterance is December 18 of that same year. A bare sixteen weeks of prophetic activity, but it was enough to get the job done. The Temple was begun. It got finished. These scant few verses, the second shortest book in the Old Testament, contain the sum and total of the prophecies of Haggai. It's not much, but a pebble gets an avalanche started.

And it doesn't hurt if the prophet gets involved. The scripture from Ezra notes that "with them were the prophets of God, helping them." This may mean that Haggai picked up a few rocks himself. It never hurts for the leader to work the hardest.

Most of all, he got the people to work. Work is ownership. Work is fellowship. When the church hires someone to build the new Christian Education wing, it may get built better, but when church members build it themselves, they become committed to the church and each other.

It's called "sweat equity." The Habitat for Humanity program understands that. Habitat uses volunteer labor to build affordable homes for the poor. No matter how unskilled, the new owners are expected to work on the home as well. It has helped ensure a near 100 percent success rate when it comes to meeting the mortgage.

So what is the significance of this prophet and his work? Some have complained that Haggai's vision was limited to the Temple, to a building. Considering the fact that Jesus was singularly unimpressed by this building some centuries later when his disciples oohed and aahed, and went so far as to tell his listeners that a better temple would be destroyed and rebuilt in three days, we may wonder what relevance these words have for us.

But Haggai's significance extends far beyond the building he encouraged. His work was essential. He helped to *redefine the kingdom of God.*

Although the people returned to the land, it was not as members of an autonomous nation, but as a province among provinces. They were no longer ruled by a king, but by a governor.

Zerubbabel was that governor. Appointed by Darius, he was the grandson of a king, but no king himself. Though he was of the lineage of King David, his name meant "seed of Babylon." Born in a foreign land, he was probably Babylonian in culture and upbringing, although he no doubt identified with his people. Though he had responsibility over the province, he had no real authority. Darius had the authority.

Haggai came to remind Zerubbabel and the people that Darius might have the appearance of authority, but "the word of the LORD" takes precedence. His book reminds us that God is ruler over the nations. God is looking ahead to a different kind of kingdom, a kingdom that will last forever. It will be ruled by a son of David, but one who is eternal.

Haggai might have been talking about a temple, but he was looking beyond to a much more glorious structure — the manger of Bethlehem. How much of this Haggai clearly saw is debatable, but the fact remains he was looking ahead to the king of glory, and the first step, as far as he could tell, was to get up and do something. No more excuses. Just do something. Take a large task and break it down into smaller tasks. Get started.

This is something that is easy to forget. The job ahead can seem so complicated, the work of the kingdom so daunting, that we are tempted to give up.

Which of us, for example, can solve world hunger? On the other hand, most of us can spend a few hours in a soup kitchen or gathering groceries for the local food pantry. Most of us can't rescue a nation, but we can write a check that fits our budget to send to our denominational hunger programs.

For sixteen years the people of Israel had done very little towards rebuilding the kingdom. Along came a prophet who spoke for barely sixteen weeks. He made a permanent mark.

Emotionally it is easier to commit for the short term. Many times we think a commitment to the church has to be lifelong. If we're a Sunday school teacher once, we serve for life. Board chair once, board chair for eternity. Sometimes the greatest service we can do for the church is to fill in at the right moment. And the short-term ministry can be terrifically significant.

Haggai is a prophet for the moment, like us. He's a Not Ready for Prime Time Prophet. There's none of the heady poetry of other prophetic books, none of the grandiose visions of, say, his contemporary, Zechariah. Haggai speaks in prose, but he speaks in time. He believes heaven and earth are connected, one kingdom. What's done on earth is reflected in heaven. What's done in the divine realm has an effect here. There's room in the prophetic kingdom for those who know how to use a hammer. At least it's doing something.

Haggai's name means "Feast" or "Holiday." There is a suggestion of dancing and music to the root word as well. Some have suggested he was born near the Feast of Booths, which is like Family Camp, when everyone would take to tents and rough it for a while. Getting down and dirty is also good fellowship. Like hard work, it bonds people together.

A prophet's larger vision is essential. I'm reminded of the old story of the traveler who arrived at a medieval town. He found one man scowling, breaking big rocks into smaller rocks. "What are you doing?" asked the traveler. "Breaking rocks," grunted the worker.

A little further down the road the traveler came upon another man performing the exact same task, but this fellow was whistling.

When asked what he was doing, the second worker smiled and said, "I'm building a cathedral."

Vision of the larger things helps us make sense of our smaller tasks.

And if it hadn't worked out? If Haggai hadn't measured up? If this prophet for the moment hesitated a second and missed out? That's our fear many times. That we will undertake a work on the part of the church and fall short.

Well, Haggai didn't work alone. Zechariah the prophet is his contemporary, and to a large extent overshadows him. His visions and dreams not only shaped the Temple, but the vision of the suffering servant. No prophet is more quoted during the gospel sections on the death of Jesus than Zechariah.

The pressure is off. God wants to use us, but he's got contingency plans. He knows we're only human, and if we are called to be his emissary for that time, whether in the Christian Education department, on the Trustee Commission, or in the other ministries of the church, rest assured that God is calling many people. We are allowed to fail because God's will SHALL be done.

The word of the Lord came by the prophet Haggai. That word told a people that God's kingdom is eternal, and forever, and the line of David would not fail, even though there was no longer a Davidic king, and the current governor, Zerubbabel, would be the last Davidic governor. O come, all ye faithful, joyful and triumphant. Be building Jerusalem, but look to Bethlehem.

Something better is coming, something beyond our wildest expectations. The king of glory is on his way. It is he who is in charge, not Darius, not Caesar, not any worldly ruler.

As Eugene Petersen puts it in *The Message*, his translation of the New Testament, "Are you listening to this? Really listening?" (Mark 4:23). Or as you may remember it, "Let those who have ears to hear, hear."

While This House
Lies In Ruins

---

*Thus says the LORD of hosts: These people say the time
has not yet come to rebuild the Lord's house. Then the
word of the LORD came by the prophet Haggai, saying:
Is it a time for you yourselves to live in your paneled
houses, while this house lies in ruins?*

*Now therefore thus says the LORD of hosts: Consider
how you have fared. You have sown much, and harvested
little; you eat, but you never have enough; you drink, but
you never have your fill; you clothe yourselves, but no
one is warm; and you that earn wages earn wages to put
them into a bag with holes.*

*Thus says the LORD of hosts: Consider how you have
fared. Go up to the hills and bring wood and build the
house, so that I may take pleasure in it and be honored,
says the LORD. You have looked for much, and, lo, it
came to little; and when you brought it home, I blew it
away. Why? says the LORD of hosts. Because my house
lies in ruins, while all of you hurry off to your own houses.*

*Therefore the heavens above you have withheld the
dew, and the earth has withheld its produce. And I have
called for a drought on the land and the hills, on the grain,
the new wine, the oil, on what the soil produces, on human beings and animals, and on all their labors.*

*Then Zerubbabel son of Shealtiel, and Joshua son of
Jehozadak, the high priest, with all the remnant of the
people, obeyed the voice of the LORD their God, and the
words of the prophet Haggai, as the LORD their God
had sent him; and the people feared the LORD. Then
Haggai, the messenger of the LORD, spoke to the people*

with the Lord's message, saying, I am with you, says the
LORD.
> *And the LORD stirred up the spirit of Zerubbabel son*
> *of Shealtiel, governor of Judah, and the spirit of Joshua*
> *son of Jehozadak, the high priest, and the spirit of all the*
> *remnant of the people; and they came and worked on the*
> *house of the LORD of hosts, their God, on the twenty-*
> *fourth day of the month, in the sixth month.*

— Haggai 1:2-15

Hymnologists say the first hymn in a hymnal tells a lot about the rest of the book. Our last hymnal began with "Holy, Holy, Holy," a marvelous hymn we have retained, but it is a relic of the time when we thought we were going to be a high church.

We are not. We're just not comfortable with big city church ways. The hymnal that rests in the pews of our small country church has this for an opener:

> *What is this place where we are meeting?*
> *Only a house, the earth its floor,*
> *walls and a roof sheltering people,*
> *windows for light, an open door.*
> *Yet it becomes a body that lives*
> *When we are gathered here,*
> *and know our God is near.*

— Huub Oosterhuis, *Zomaar een dak boven wat hoofden,*
tr. by David Smith, from *Hymnal: A Worship Book*

As much as I like a large church building, with a spire, stained-glass windows, intricate wooden carvings, grand mosaics, and art work of biblical scenes, I feel most at home in a plain building. The windows are clear glass so we can see the world outside, which is our mission field. If we're going to look at anything, it is at the people around us, who are the body of Christ.

God has not needed a grand building during the course of his history with his people. During the exodus, the ark rested in what amounted to a large tent. Pick up the stakes and keep moving. Indeed, that's what the word "dwelt" is derived from, in the phrase

20

from John 1:14: "And the word was made flesh and dwelt among us." God's word became flesh and tented, or camped out, among us. There is an element of roughing it inherent in the incarnation, and the suggestion that we should continue to rough it during our pilgrimage on this earth.

When David was all on fire to build the first temple, God sent him the message just to slow down and wait a generation. And after Solomon had it built, so beautiful that it became the stuff of legend, it didn't help to make the people any holier.

The earliest Christians met in homes, and during times of persecution, the catacombs. Cathedrals didn't get built until the church got legal.

And most important of all, when Jesus came into the world, a humble manger in a stable was good enough for him. Something great and tremendous and holy was crowded into such a very small place, yet it would not have been a more magnificent event had it taken place in a palace. The shepherds, the angels, the wise men, everything about the scene was as glorious as it could be, because of the contrast between the humble and the heavenly majesty.

As we pick up with this scripture from the Book of Haggai, with its call to rebuild the Temple, we have to ask: Why is it so important? Does it matter if there is another temple, especially if, as we suggest, that God has new plans for his people?

First of all, it doesn't matter. The church is just a place. Have you ever noticed that when a church burns down, either by accident or arson, the people meet the next week in the parking lot and do just fine?

But the text itself gives a very good reason why the Temple should be rebuilt.

> *Thus says the LORD of hosts: These people say the time has not yet come to rebuild the Lord's house. Then the word of the LORD came by the prophet Haggai, saying: Is it a time for you yourselves to live in your paneled houses, while this house lies in ruins?* — Haggai 1:2-4

It is a question of justice. These people have good homes. God's house is a hovel. It wouldn't matter if everyone lived in a shack.

But if you can spend money on yourself, you can spend money on God.

To be honest, most of the people did not live in paneled houses. There was a gap between the rich and the poor. The gap persists today and it is always getting wider.

Jesus had very pointed things to say about richer believers. The prophets who pointed to Jesus also pointed at the economic injustice that was rampant in their times. Since then it has been the appointed task of preachers and teachers to point out that Jesus didn't really mean what he said about camels and needle eyes. Nonsense. Jesus and the prophets were giving a saving warning. There is nothing intrinsically wrong with money, but it can anesthetize. It can fool you into thinking you are all right, you are independent, you don't need others, and you don't need God. At least all the time.

What a deal! Think about it. The people had the best of things, and they figured someone else would take care of God's work. Maybe next year. Sixteen next years had gone by and the Temple was a shabby ruin.

The exiles complained that they didn't have time to work on the Temple, what with the day-to-day cares of living, but their own homes were well insulated against the storm.

Like eating your cake and having it, too. Praise God. When it's convenient.

It was like the practice of Korban that Jesus denounced. People set aside money for the temple to inherit when they were dead, and they lived off that money. And they did not take care of their obligations, especially with regards to taking care of their parents, because they could rightly claim that the money was set aside for God's work. After they were dead. Darn good deal. Being holy and living like the devil.

After all, sooner or later someone will take care of it. Someone else.

There is an even greater gap between God and his people. Notice the text says, "These people say...." God is not referring to them as "my people." Every generation needs a different kind of wake-up call, a different medicine. To this generation Haggai has come to say: "It is time to act like a community. It is time to build a church."

Church building is one way to build community. In the movie *Lilies of the Field* a convent of nuns has a dream of a chapel in the middle of the wilderness. But they lack a prophet; they lack a catalyst. The character played by Sidney Poitier was like Haggai. He saw that it could be done — with sweat and patience and hope. He was that someone else who took care of it. But others had to help.

Building a church isn't the only thing that can save us. But anything that causes us to look away from ourselves, away from our things, and towards other people, towards God, can do the trick. God has to do what he can to get our attention. It's that important.

Now during this time there was great strife in the world. Darius was consolidating his kingdom. Two years of brushfire wars kept him busy. Anything could happen. The whole world order could collapse. How can you possibly build a temple when so much is going on?

But as Jesus said, there will be wars and rumors of war. This sort of thing is always going on. You can't use the current political situation as an excuse, then or now. And that is why Haggai uses the phrase "Yahweh of Hosts." It occurs fourteen times in the 38 verses of Haggai. You'll find it 53 times in his contemporary, Zechariah, and 24 times in Malachi, another post-exilic prophet. They spoke to a people without a king.

Or rather, a people who forgot who the real king was all along. The Lord of Hosts is the captain of the greatest army. Whether the hosts stand for angels, stars, or the armies of Israel, the image is one of power and might. God is the real lord of history, king of kings, lord of lords.

At times of despair we may wonder: What's the use? What does it matter? God's work is the use. God's power is the matter.

It may seem like we will make little dent in world hunger, or have marginal effect on the great events of our day. But that does not excuse us from plunging in.

And we do have an effect. They say if a butterfly sneezes in Hong Kong someone in Peoria catches a cold. It's a way of saying we're all connected, especially now, when our economies overlap and no one is truly isolated. What one person does affects another, and even affects creation. Haggai asks the people to consider this:

> *Now therefore thus says the LORD of hosts: Consider how you have fared. You have sown much, and harvested little; you eat, but you never have enough; you drink, but you never have your fill; you clothe yourselves, but no one is warm; and you that earn wages earn wages to put them into a bag with holes. Thus says the LORD of hosts: Consider how you have fared.*
>
> — Haggai 1:5-7

The people are facing light harvests and tough winters. The money is losing its value. Did you honestly think, he asks, that what you do would not affect the world around you?

Before you ask if our actions really affect the weather, it is well to remember that we are changing the climate of our earth even now, widening the hole in the ozone layer, deforesting great portions of the globe, affecting the balance between carbon dioxide and oxygen. The debate is still going on as to whether we will experience another ice age or a global warming. What is certain is that our lifestyle affects the world.

Haggai is saying the same thing to the people of Israel. Your economy and your crops are suffering. Did you ever think there might be cause and effect?

It's like the Car Wash Theology, best expressed in this little song written by humorist Allan Sherman:

> *Oh, the moon is shining bright upon the car wash,*
> *So I'm having my Volkwagon washed today.*
> *But the way things go with me, the way my luck runs,*
> *Just as soon as they finish it will rain.*

Our power to affect the world around us increases when we act as a community. As a people we can seek to feed the hungry and make a difference. Or as a people we can forget the temple and see what happens.

Then Zerubbabel son of Shealtiel, and Joshua son of Jehozadak, the high priest, with all the remnant of the people, obeyed the voice of the LORD their God, and the words of the prophet Haggai, as the LORD their God had sent him; and the people feared the LORD. Then Haggai, the messenger of the LORD, spoke to the people with the Lord's message, saying, I am with you, says the LORD. And the LORD stirred up the spirit of Zerubbabel son of Shealtiel, governor of Judah, and the spirit of Joshua son of Jehozadak, the high priest, and the spirit of all the remnant of the people; and they came and worked on the house of the LORD of hosts, their God, on the twenty-fourth day of the month, in the sixth month.

— Haggai 1:12-15

In my church we have all Indians and no chiefs. By that I mean to say that if one person will take on the mantle of leadership, he or she will never have to lift a finger. There are so many willing workers that jobs get done in a moment. But it is like pulling teeth to get that one chief!

Haggai takes on the job of chief. And the people respond. The response is enthusiastic, and seems to be unanimous. Haggai, like the Sidney Poitier character, works with the people. He sweats with the rest of them.

And a great thing happens. God no longer speaks of "these people." He says, "I am with you." They came and got the job done.

The remnant is found. There is always a remnant, a portion of God's people waiting to be called out of the chaos, ready to take up the gauntlet, ready to work for the kingdom. No matter how fallen the age, there is always a remnant of ordinary people who will work great wonders for the Lord.

Most important of all, the stage is set. Literally. This is *the* Temple. Yes, it will be desecrated and partially destroyed by the Selucid Empire in the second century B.C. and require restoration by Herod the Great. Essentially, however, this is the one. This temple which they have begun to build will be the setting for the holy family when Jesus is presented in the Temple. "Now you can let your servant depart in peace," Simeon will say, and Anna will echo, "Amen!"

The twelve-year-old Jesus will find his way here while his parents leave home for Nazareth, teaching the teachers, recognizing the work of his Father.

And this is the place that Jesus will cleanse, casting out the money changers. Here he will debate the scribes and pharisees. And at this site he will identify the true temple, his body which will be broken for many for the forgiveness of sins, which will be destroyed and rebuilt in three days. How could those workers know that the most important result of their work wouldn't happen for five and a half centuries?

One time at my church in Los Angeles I received what I thought was an odd revelation. A grand "What If," if you will. I passed it on to the congregation.

I pointed out to them that a woman from another church had served as our nursery school director for about a year. It was a short stewardship, and she worked there to earn money to pay for the costs of an adoption.

"Wouldn't it be strange," I said one Sunday, "if God's reason for this church, all its struggles and triumphs, had been to make it possible for these parents and this child to get together?" I'm not saying that's so. Yet the idea came to me from outside. It's worth considering. It put all of our pride and prejudice in a different perspective.

I wouldn't put it past God. Stranger things have taken place.

Either way, next time there's a temple to be built, put the challenge to the people. Don't assume they won't help. Let them respond. Prepare to be surprised.

This House
In Its Former Glory

---

*In the second year of King Darius, in the seventh month,
on the twenty-first day of the month, the word of the LORD
came by the prophet Haggai, saying: Speak now to Zerubbabel son of Shealtiel, governor of Judah, and to Joshua
son of Jehozadak, the high priest, and to the remnant of
the people, and say, Who is left among you that saw this
house in its former glory? How does it look to you now?
Is it not in your sight as nothing?*

*Yet now take courage, O Zerubbabel, says the LORD;
take courage, O Joshua, son of Jehozadak, the high priest;
take courage, all you people of the land, says the LORD;
work, for I am with you, says the LORD of hosts, accord-
ing to the promise that I made you when you came out of
Egypt. My spirit abides among you; do not fear.*

*For thus says the LORD of hosts: Once again, in a
little while, I will shake the heavens and the earth and the
sea and the dry land; and I will shake all the nations, so
that the treasure of all nations shall come, and I will fill
this house with splendor, says the LORD of hosts.*

*The silver is mine, and the gold is mine, says the LORD
of hosts. The latter splendor of this house shall be greater
than the former, says the LORD of hosts; and in this place
I will give prosperity, says the LORD of hosts.*

— Haggai 2:1-9

One summer we took a long family vacation, traveling from
Elkhart, Indiana, west to Grants Pass, Oregon, south to Los Angeles, and ending in Silver City, New Mexico, before heading back
for the Midwest.

Three weeks and six thousand miles, and only three nights in motels. Otherwise we depended on the kindness of friends and relatives.

The trip started with cool weather. I wore sweatshirts in Oregon to the outdoor theater in Ashland. By the time we hit L.A., with the World Cup in full swing, it was hot. We survived Disneyland. Then it got hotter.

By the time we began the drive to New Mexico it was baking: 126 degrees, even hotter than the 122 we encountered four years earlier on a similar trip. It's hard to describe just how hot hot can be. The air conditioning ran full blast in the car and we were still uncomfortable. When we stopped at a rest stop my movements were stiff and uncertain. I felt like I was walking through hot, dry sponges.

We spent the night with a good friend who lived near Florence, Arizona. Thank heavens for her air conditioning. The next morning we stopped to get a look at the Casa Grande ruins. We baked in the sun. There was no one nearby. The single building was said to be the site of what was once a thriving Native American settlement. Hard to believe it was still standing, but we were told the supporting beams had been dragged from hundreds of miles away, and they still provided support.

Ruins.

A couple days later we took a side trip from Silver City. It takes two and a half hours to drive around forty miles along State Road 15, said to be the worst road in New Mexico. That's how you get to the remote Gila Indian Cliff Dwellings of the Mogollon Indians. Tall firs jut out from the steep sides of sheer cliffs. Like pipe cleaners the fir and pine stand erect on the edge. Don't look down if you get giddy.

The caves themselves were nearly inaccessible to tourists until steps were cemented into the hillsides not long ago. Into these natural caves the Mogollon Indians carried mortar and stones to build walls, graineries, and fire pits. It's hard to draw your breath when you're a mile high in altitude. A lonely wind blew; a hawk played on the drafts.

This enterprise was not intended as a lonely outpost, but as a home for families, a dwelling for generations and generations. People had lived here once upon a time. Seven hundred years ago they built.

The settlement lasted forty years. They left, never to return. Did the soil grow infertile? Was the ecology disturbed? Were there social problems? No one knows. The wind blows through the pines; the birds soar on the updrafts.

Ruins.

I love ruins. I've stood next to Roman walls in London and near the great monument at Stonehenge. I've walked among the remains of the California Missions along the Camino Real.

But ruins are deceiving. People don't live in ruins. They live in buildings. When you look at ruins it can be hard to imagine what the place was like when it was thriving. It was hard to picture a place filled with people when it was home.

You have to imagine the place crawling with kids, and people hollering or laughing, men and women arm in arm. But it's hard.

More likely you imagine giants walking among the stones. Not people like you and me.

This is part of what happened, I think, when the exiles walked among the ruins of the old Temple. It was not a place for the living. It daunted. Their homes were scattered all around it, and there it stood, taunting them. We were glory, it seemed to say. You, of a lesser generation, are nothing. Like it says in the Bible, "There were giants in the earth in those days ... the same became mighty men who were of old, men of renown" (Genesis 6:4, KJV).

Yet the ones who built the Temple were people. Humans. It's dangerous to assume otherwise. I'm sure this is one of the reasons Jesus picked such ordinary people for apostles. He didn't want us to have an excuse when it came to following in his footsteps. The apostles and disciples achieved great things, stared into the face of death, and accepted martyrdom. But the stories in the Gospels make it clear they were just regular folks. It is God who is revealed in our weakness.

In what they imagined were the shadows of giants, those who had returned from exile wondered how they could possibly match

29

the Temple's former glory. They got to work right away under the direction of Haggai and Zechariah, Zerubbabel and Joshua. They responded to the words of accusation. Now, perhaps as they began to lose heart, it was time for words of encouragement. God sent those words.

The oracle in this text is, like the previous one, well dated. October 17, in the year 520, barely a couple of weeks after God had declared that this was his people and he would be with them, God spoke again.

The Feast of Booths had already been celebrated. This annual harvest event was like family camp. People gathered outside the city and set up tents, roughing it for a few days. Kids loved it, I'm sure, and so did all the other outdoor types. The rest no doubt endured it, in good humor or not. It is important for us to be taken out of our regular routine, to be reminded we are sojourners, and not to get too comfortable.

The people had been pushed out of their comfort zone anyway, in responding to the prophecy and setting aside time to work on the Temple. Now, only three days from Yom Kippur, a time of introspection when the community confessed their sins, God speaks.

Who is left among you that saw this house in its former glory? How does it look to you now? Is it not in your sight as nothing? — Haggai 2:3

That doesn't sound encouraging, to be sure, but it is a statement of fact. There were those who probably had seen the Temple in its former glory — but they must have been very old. The sharpest memories of the elderly are often those associated with their childhood and youth. These men and women could vividly recall the sights and sounds of the old Temple. And they could see that the new one did not measure up.

But as accurate as childhood memories can be, they are flawed. Not because they are incorrect. They are too correct. I'll try to explain.

My son Jacob is the youngest of three children. He used to accompany me as I dropped off first his older brother, and then his

30

older sister, at the local kindergarten. Normally I'm fairly permissive, but I would not allow him to use the playground equipment because I wanted to save an experience for him to look forward to when he finally went there himself.

For him the holy grail was the elephant slide. Actually, it was a regular slide, but there were metal sidings on both sides that were painted to look like elephants. It looked so tall and magnificent. Jacob could hardly wait for his turn.

The day came at last and we walked together into the schoolyard. He ran through the playground for the elephant slide, then came to an abrupt stop. Turning to me with a puzzled expression, he asked, "Hey, who shortened the slide?"

No one had shortened the slide. Over the space of three years he'd grown, and his perspective had changed!

In the same way the survivors of the exile, who had been taken away as young children, remembered the Temple through the eyes of the very young. Everything looked bigger than real. No wonder the Temple looked like nothing in their sight!

Nothing measures up to the good old days, but they weren't as good as we imagined. People who talk about going back to the pre-Industrial Revolution forget how disease and drudgery drained individuals, who died early and often. They forget the high infant mortality rate, and the fact that most of us were servants or serfs and not the well off. They forget the Middle Ages were the thousand years without a bath, and that ignorance led people to kill cats as servants of the devil, so mice ran free, spreading the plague. People forget.

So God says, "Yet now take courage, all you people of the land ... Work, for I am with you."

The people are to have confidence in this statement because they have a God with a history. The reference to "the promise that I made you when you came out of Egypt" reminds them that they are a people who are set apart. They should have been no people, but they are now God's people. When Moses asks for God's name, he tells him, "I am that I am," and he goes on to say that he is the God of Abraham, of Isaac, of Jacob. We know God, and people, because of the history we share. Names don't mean as much as action.

We as Christians were once no people, but God called us into existence as one people, God's people, drawn from every nation on the globe.

These things will come, God says, "Once again, in a little while." It is the Lord of Hosts who says this, the captain of the army of the Lord. This figure appears to Joshua the night before the battle of Jericho. Not realizing he is standing in the presence of God, Joshua asks the figure whose side he is on. God identifies himself as the captain of the army of the Lord, and Joshua realizes the real question is not whether God is on our side, but whether we are on God's side.

Wait. "Michael shall arise!" we are assured by the prophet Daniel (Daniel 12:1).

This book, reflecting experiences from the exile through the mirror of the Selucid occupation that would come in the second century before Christ, spoke to a people horribly oppressed with the message: Wait. Soon and very soon we are going to see the king. God's army will appear and set the world on its ear. The last shall be first. These will be events of earthshaking significance. This won't be something that takes place in an obscure province on the edge of an empire. This will be immediately evident to all. Every nation shall know about it, and the center of the universe will be God's people. No one will be unaffected. "I will shake all the nations, so that the treasure of all the nations shall come, and I will fill this house with splendor" (Haggai 2:7).

That is the great encouragement. In the end our efforts need not be sufficient. God will make up the difference. He justifies us, thank heavens, because we always fall short.

"Once again, in a little while I will shake the heavens and the sea and the land." Our God is a God of power, an active God who promises to reorder everything. The treasure belongs to God, even if his sovereignty is not recognized by others. "The silver is mine, and the gold is mine, says the Lord of hosts." Don't forget it.

Overlooked sometimes is the fact that it will take the treasure of the nations to make the temple complete. The call to the nations went out even before the birth of Jesus, in the form of a star.

It would take a book to tell the whole story, but suffice it to say that those commentaries that date the birth of Jesus between 4 and 7 B.C. are wrong.

In 3 B.C. the decree went out requiring Mary and Joseph to register in Bethlehem. Herod the Great died mad between the Lunar Eclipse of January 9, 1 B.C., and the Passover which began on April 8 of that year.

And in between, on August 12, 3 B.C., the Magi watched Jupiter and Venus, the King and Queen of Heaven, seem to touch in the sky near the king star Regulus, in the constellation of Leo, which was associated with the tribe of Judah.

Twice more (February 17, 2 B.C., and May 8, 2 B.C.) this formation recurred. The Magi set out to seek the king. And a century later the martyr Ignatius wrote regarding this story, "Thence was destroyed all magic, and every bond vanished; evil's ignorance was abolished, the old kingdom perished, God being revealed as human to bring newness of Eternal Life."

God is calling us into one community. We are not complete unless all the nations are gathered together. Considering that the church remains the most segregated of social institutions, with the segregation enforced by all sides, it becomes clear this unity will take place only at the command and the timing of God. It is not something we seem to be able to accomplish on our own. But in order for the temple to be fully outfitted, in order for the church to be presented as the holy bride of Christ, we must be made whole in all our limbs, and can no longer remain separate peoples. It will take all our treasure to make this a holy place.

Outside there are revolutions and the empire is unsettled. Darius is setting the house in order. But here there is a great task to be done. It is a call to action, to rebuilding the community, in this instance through the temple. The temple we are called to build is the body of Christ, and it includes people of every ethnic, social, economic, and chronologic class.

But it is hard to remember that when you are building the temple and it doesn't measure up with your dreams.

I think back to my days in school. I have always had a way with words, but I can't draw a straight line. It was a source of constant frustration to me that I couldn't draw what I saw in my head. My drawings in school never measured up to my standards, but they were plenty good enough for my parents, who displayed them proudly. God is proud of our efforts, recognizing our limitations — and our potential — as well.

I call to mind this story every time I think things were better in the old days.

Once a local radio station in Los Angeles sponsored an essay contest. There were twelve first prizes offered to the general public. A trip for two to London, Frankfurt, or New York. I wanted to go to London very badly. Pen in hand, I wrote out what I thought was a super first draft. Setting it aside in order to gain objectivity, I returned to my efforts a week later, only to discover I couldn't find the draft.

Because the deadline was so near I waved my arms around in frustration, but finally settled down and wrote out a new draft. It wasn't very good, in my estimation, not compared to the first one, but it was all I had. I turned it in.

I won.

My wife and I had a marvelous trip to London, extending the trip so we could visit Scotland and other parts of England as well.

Months later I found that original first draft. The page had slipped under a heavy piece of furniture.

It was awful. It was nowhere near as good as my later effort. If I had submitted it, I'm not sure I'd have won.

"The latter splendor of this house shall be greater than the former, says the Lord of hosts; and in this place I will give prosperity, says the Lord of hosts."

Got that? Things just get better. Even when it seems like it is all falling apart, trust God, and wait. Michael shall arise!

Those ruins are a shadow. The real temple is being built.

And still stands.

The building raised by Haggai's contemporaries was the stage on which Jesus stood, while warning of a greater temple that would be destroyed and rebuilt in three days. And he shall reign forever and ever.

Take heart. God is on our side. He will give this place prosperity. Eternally. Thus says the Lord of Hosts.

Yes, It
Becomes Unclean

Thus says the LORD of hosts: Ask the priests for a ruling: If one carries consecrated meat in the fold of one's garment, and with the fold touches bread, or stew, or wine, or oil, or any kind of food, does it become holy? The priests answered, "No."

Then Haggai said, "If one who is unclean by contact with a dead body touches any of these, does it become unclean?" The priests answered, "Yes, it becomes unclean."

Haggai then said, So is it with this people, and with this nation before me, says the LORD; and so with every work of their hands; and what they offer there is unclean. But now, consider what will come to pass from this day on. Before a stone was placed upon a stone in the Lord's temple, how did you fare? When one came to a heap of twenty measures, there were but ten; when one came to the winevat to draw fifty measures, there were but twenty. I struck you and all the products of your toil with blight and mildew and hail; yet you did not return to me, says the LORD.   — Haggai 2:11-17

When my family grew large enough, not so much in numbers, but in the size of its members, it was time to get a van. We have been a one-car family for most of two decades, so we've had to fit in whatever vehicle we owned. There was a time when one of those nice little yuppie station wagons did the trick.

Remember the old station wagons, which were half the size of an aircraft carrier? Looking back from the front seat to the back you could see a person's lips move and it still took half a second for the sound to reach you. But the little station wagons were compact and gave the illusion of space. Until the kids grew up.

So we had a minivan, because like most of the people of our generation, we didn't want to admit that what we really needed was a caravan of wagons in order to separate the kids and keep them from fighting. The minivans came with automatic transmissions, which meant saying good-bye to that comforting stick shift.

I like manual transmission, because even though I don't know a thing about engines and my wife is the only one of us who has actually changed the oil, moving that stick shift around helps me pretend I know about cars.

So after a four-and-a-half-year absence it was nice to buy a small economy car with a manual transmission. Brrrrrrr-rum! I hummed to myself, mimicking the sound of the engine. First to second gear. Brrrrrrr-rum! Second to third.

My oldest son was now old enough to drive, and that meant he was stuck with the van, because the manual transmission can be confusing to a beginner. Teaching anyone to drive is confusing, especially because you discover you don't know English anymore.

"Do that," you instruct from the passenger's seat, as doom approaches.

"What that? This that?"

"No! That that."

Directions are even worse.

"Turn left?" the driver asks.

"Right." You answer.

"Back up?" the driver asks.

"Go ahead!" you reply.

Not much communication there.

"Turn left?" should be answered by "Yes, turn left!" Be specific. That way there is no confusion.

And to avoid confusion, Haggai, in this section of the prophecy, asks yes and no questions to make his point. This is where we all get off the train.

This is when things get just a little boring, thank you very much. Most people consider the law to be the most tedious section of Scripture. You start with the marvelous stories of Genesis and the

Exodus from Egypt, but then, in the barren wastes between Exodus 20 and the death of Moses in Deuteronomy, Bible readers get lost in the desert waste of the Law. Please, tell us about the baby Jesus. Or the baby Moses. Or even Elisha. Anything but this.

Some people just skim this stuff. I encourage it, actually. In coaching members of my church in a read through the Bible program, I told them they had my permission to skim through Leviticus. Let your eyes wander over the page, I said, and see if they light on an interesting verse. Otherwise, process, but don't absorb the words.

I feel guilty doing this, but I know how many good intentions have been ended by Numbers and Deuteronomy, how many resolutions to get through all of God's word have run into the brick wall of the Law.

Yet to me these are some of the best parts. The Law contains our highest aspirations, our desire to answer the challenge to be holy and separate as a people, to mimic God, to present ourselves as the pure bride of Christ. We know now we're incapable of it, that we need the help of God to be made righteous enough to be brought into his presence. But it's a nice idea.

Fortunately, most of the boring stuff is quarantined in the first five books of the Bible, but there is a sprinkling of it throughout the Old Testament. Like this section in the book of Haggai.

When Haggai and the priests begin to discuss the concept of clean and unclean, many get a glassy-eyed expression. Yet this is an important concept. It reminds us that we are a people, and not just individuals.

Clean and unclean mean different things to different people. It changes from society to society, and has little to do with how clean our hands are so much as how we clean our hands. In some cultures, eating with the left hand is unthinkable! We don't care. We're more likely to argue over the method we use to wash our dishes. One way gets them clean. Another appalls us, even though the dishes are perfectly sanitized.

Originally, being unclean was not considered a moral flaw. There was the recognition that after working with sick people, or burying the dead, or performing other functions, a little time was needed for purification before returning to the community. There was nothing wrong with you personally.

But over time God's people had built up elaborate rules for clean and unclean, some of them nearly ridiculous. No matter what you did, you were excluded from the community because you were unclean. And suddenly judgment was involved.

When the Pharisees asked Jesus why his disciples didn't practice cleanliness, he went to the root of the problem. It's not what goes into the mouth, but what comes out which makes us unclean. It's what is in the heart — which is what God originally intended for his people anyway.

Still, the array of laws can be very confusing. Rules for rashes, rules for infections, rules for mildew on clothes and in the very stones of the walls — it can be a little numbing. Rules for this and rules for that — what meaning can these laws have for the modern Christian?

But then you remember, the children of Israel were a pilgrim people bound together by a covenant. They were on their way to the promised land, and once they arrived they were supposed to be the light for the nations.

And it's true. What infects one infects all. The laws of health begin to make sense.

We are still a pilgrim people, bound together in the body of Christ, as we journey towards the kingdom. One body. The Law reminds us there are no "victimless" crimes, that our own personal pollution infects and affects everyone around us. We are one in the spirit, one in the Lord, and we need to take stock of the four walls of our own temple.

As the poet John Donne wrote many centuries ago in his seventeenth Meditation, "No man is an island, entire of itself; every man is a piece of the continent, a part of the main." We are all connected to each other. The blight of the nation's inner cities cannot be ignored by those who live in rural counties, just as the problems of the farmers must concern the white-collar worker on the eightieth floor of a bank building. Even national borders are no protection. One nation's economic difficulty affects us all.

The people who have begun rebuilding the Temple are coming off a time of famine, wondering why this has occurred. The best way for God to explain this is to ask the priests a couple of questions through Haggai.

The first question is: "If one carries consecrated meat in the fold of one's garment, and the fold touches bread, or stew, or wine, or oil, or any kind of food, does it become holy?"

The answer the priests give is a simple no.

Haggai is asking yes or no questions because he is building a case. He doesn't want comment from his listeners. He wants to lead them somewhere with their consent.

Sanctity, Haggai is suggesting, has always been seen as something that is difficult to acquire. It cannot be passed on. Each individual as well, in order to become holy, or separate, must dedicate oneself to achieving this goal. I've heard it put this way: "God has no grandchildren." We may all be children of God, but none of us inherits this condition. We join the family by choice.

Haggai's next question, "If one who is unclean by contact with a dead body touches any of these, does it become unclean?" requires a yes answer. When you drop food on a dirty floor, it becomes as dirty as the floor. Every cook knows this. Most of us don't really have floors clean enough to eat off of, and even if we did, most of us wouldn't eat off the floor anyway. That's what ritually unclean is all about.

But Hebrew does not have a way of simply saying yes. Just as you answer the driver's question of "Turn left?" with the answer, "Yes, turn left," instead of "Right! Oops, I mean correct!"; so also in order to give an affirmative answer in Hebrew you have to speak in a complete sentence that affirms the question. The priests therefore reply, "Yes, it becomes unclean."

There can be no doubt in the answer. This is the way we expect things to happen.

But now Haggai begins to give us an idea of the new covenant that will be revealed with Jesus.

He asks the people to consider: Before they laid a stone in the foundation, what happened? Just as they were unclean, so everything else was unclean. When they ignored the Lord, the earth itself ignored them. Crops were only half as bountiful as expected, and blight, mildew, and hail hampered their efforts.

But in one of those delightful biblical paradoxes, the Lord tells the people that clean made the unclean clean (say that five times fast) when they laid that foundation stone. "Consider from this day on, from the twenty-fourth day of the ninth month," writes Haggai. The effort the people made, turning away from their problems, to serve God in building the Temple, has led to seed in the barn and fruit on the vine.

As Jesus put it, "With God all things are possible." So during his ministry when the woman with a flow of blood touched his hem she was healed. She was unclean by her people's standards, and Jesus should have been made unclean by touching her. Just the opposite occurred. He noted that his power seemed to flow from himself to her.

An even better example might be the encounter between Jesus and the Samaritan woman. The Samaritans, remember, were those believers who were left behind during the exile, too poor and destitute to matter. When the generation of the exile arrived, years before Haggai's prophecies, the returnees rejected the remnant in a highhanded fashion. Centuries of bitterness followed as both Jews and Samaritans claimed to be the true faith.

When Jesus spoke to the Samaritan woman he broke several barriers. He was not only speaking to a woman, who was less than a person in his society, he was speaking to a Samaritan, which would have scandalized his contemporaries and certainly made his disciples very uncomfortable. Moreover, he was asking to drink from her water jug. This was also shocking.

Yet through his actions not only was this woman made righteous, but many in her village as well.

Just as the Law was written for a people who are one body, so too Jesus came to bring all peoples into one body. We are cleansed by our association with him, washed in the blood, and saved by grace. Jesus turns things around so we infect each other with goodness.

Surely you have known people who could brighten a room by their presence. They may have born on their bodies the marks of

Christ, having endured tremendous suffering or sorrow, but they have through the Spirit the ability to elevate those around them, to inspire them to greater holiness, to cleanse the unclean.

The laying of the foundation stone made Haggai's people clean. Jesus Christ is the new foundation, the one foundation, the true cornerstone that was rejected by others, which supports the whole edifice, cleanses the whole body, redeems the entire creation.

One more note. Prior to this prophecy, Zechariah began his parallel ministry with Haggai, exhorting the people to faithfulness through attention to God's temple. Far from supplanting Haggai, the new prophet complemented his work. It's difficult to be a lone gun. If you have ever taken a stand in a church, prophesying in the name of the Lord, you may know that it is a relief when someone else rises to stand alongside you.

Next time a prophet rises among you, consider doing as Zechariah did and joining the great work. But be warned! Haggai's ministry was short-term. The new prophet's work lasted much longer, was more detailed and in some ways significant. God has a way of doing things that way!

On The
Twenty-fourth Day

On the twenty-fourth day of the ninth month, in the sec-
ond year of Darius, the word of the LORD came by the
prophet Haggai ...   — Haggai 2:10

Haggai works his way to this crucial question, and so shall we. Once again he begins a prophecy with a precise date.

These dates are nearly unique in scripture. Zechariah, Haggai's contemporary, also uses exact dates, but in most instances the date of a particular passage in the Bible is determined from outside evidence. Archaeological evidence in the form of inscriptions can sometimes provide a date for one of the Hebrew chronicles. Sometimes grammatical clues, such as the use of certain words or phrases, give scholars a rough estimate of the date of composition.

But Haggai dates his prophecies by pagan reckoning, and this allows an unusual accuracy in dating the passages.

The twenty-fourth day of the ninth month corresponds to the eighteenth day of the twelfth month in our reckoning. On December 18 in 520, near the time of the winter's solstice, the word of the Lord came to Haggai.

This word of encouragement came about the time we celebrate Christmas, at the time when the days are as short as they are going to get.

This particular season has always had a fascination for the human mind. For us it is an interesting time. Fall is beautiful, and in some ways a relief after the blistering heat and humidity which can accompany a rough summer. Fall means getting out those comfortable sweaters and sweatshirts and putting away the lawn mower.

Day and night are roughly equal, the harvest is winding down, we have canned about all we're going to can, and we've earned a rest.

But the winter's solstice is a sign that cold days are on the way, weeks without the sun, trouble with the car or the insulation or the furnace.

In the ancient world there were many who worried and wondered if this might be the end, if this would be the year the tide did not turn, but the world returned to chaos, night swallowing all as the days finally ebbed to nothing. When the days began to grow longer bit by bit, when the confirmation came that even though bitter cold lay ahead spring would someday return, the ancients celebrated.

The Israelites believed in an assurance their pagan neighbors did not share — that, as God had told Noah, "... summer and winter, springtime and harvest, will not cease."

This love affair with the solstice, falling as it will on December 20, 21, or 22, is something we baptized when we left behind our pagan past and joined Haggai as part of God's family.

It seems like every Christmas I hear someone complain about the pagan customs of Christmas. The trees are Germanic and pagan; the laurel and the holly wreaths are Roman and pagan; the date is ancient and pagan.

I say bless them all. That's the beauty of our faith. We baptize our pagan past and bring it along with us! Eggs for easter, and bunnies? Sure. The signs of spring and fertility make sense as we celebrate rebirth and resurrection.

That's the neat thing about our faith. We give up everything to follow Christ, and God gives it all back to us, in its proper perspective. Money, food, sex, and television — there's nothing intrinsically evil about any of those things, although all of them can lead us to perdition if we make an idol of them.

But put them in their proper place, behind the worship of God, and you can keep them all. Eating your cake and having it too.

From the very beginning Christians dragged along their old life and saw it made new. The only problem seems to have been the tendency to permit our own pagan past and to deny the same privilege to others.

Efforts to purify Christmas are laughable — in retrospect. For a time the grinches have their way. During the Puritan era the Ham Police roamed the streets of London, sniffing the air for evidence of a holiday revel. If a family was discovered cooking a feast for Christmas, the ham was confiscated and the people were thrown in jail!

But, as Dr. Seuss pointed out in his delightful little book *How the Grinch Stole Christmas*, the Grinch didn't stop "... Christmas from coming. It came. Somehow or other it came just the same."

Germanic Christians, English Christians, Italian Christians, all have their own customs. When African Christians or Asian Christians or Native American Christians join the fellowship some people are uncomfortable with their pagan customs, now newly baptized. God is no more European than African, and is no less pleased with the fire of our African brethren as he is with the quiet pew perchers of Europe.

As we approach Christmas, let us examine our customs, acknowledge their origins, and praise God for the new fire that burns brightly among us, reflecting the glory of the creator, as he brings us together into one family.

The nations are coming to the temple. They are bringing the treasure of their customs to share at the altar.

Is There Any Seed Left In The Barn?

Is there any seed left in the barn? Do the vine, the fig tree, the pomegranate, and the olive tree still yield nothing? From this day on I will bless you. — Haggai 2:19

About eight years ago I first considered moving from Los Angeles to northern Indiana, from the city to the country. I'm a city boy, born and bred, and I still love the city, but I thought to be fair to my children they should experience both ways of living. So we loaded up the truck and we moved to a mildly rural place called Dunlap, located halfway between Elkhart and Goshen, Indiana.

I say mildly rural because the Concord Mall is only a mile and a half north of us, but we're surrounded by cornfields and the stars shine brightly by night.

One of the things I promised myself was that when I moved to the country I would keep bees. I'm not sure why. I can take or leave honey. I can't abide bugs. But there seemed something very domestic about keeping bees, and I liked the sound of it.

The more I read, the better I liked the prospect. Gardeners work from April to October. The average hive takes less than eight hours of maintenance per year. And the bees do all the work. It seemed a win-win situation.

Once I moved out there was nothing for it but to get started. We arrived in September, too late for bee season, but I'd done my reading and research. Over the winter I ordered a basic bee hive kit and nailed the darn thing together. Nothing to it. Even the handyman-impaired like me could do it.

The frames were a little trickier, but I even got them strung with wire and arranged a foundation for the bees to build on. Come March and I got the outside painted.

Then I ordered the bees. I'd read all about installing the bees, so I figured this would be a snap.

One day I got a phone call from the post office. Come down and pick up your bees. We're not delivering them. The big day had come.

What I got was this box that consisted of a wood frame and mesh sides. It was packed with thousands of buzzing bees. When I gingerly picked it up, the buzzes rose a pitch. They were not happy.

Right then I considered whether I ought to follow Plan A (store the bees in a cool, dark place all day and feed them sugar water, so they'd be tanked up before I donned bee gear and to remove the queen, allowing a few others to fly around my head while I installed her, and then dump all the bees like so much cornflakes in the hive before closing it up) or Plan B (chuck the thing in the ditch and drive home).

I finally decided on Plan A, but I really thought about it.

I got it done too, although I was so tense at the thought of dealing with so many bees that I ended up with a stiff back for the first and so far only time in my life. I don't mean a little sore. I mean I could hardly move for a whole week.

Later it got easier. I relaxed more. I got stung some, too. But for seven years in a row I've kept bees, and even occasionally harvested some honey.

One tough question I always face is, do the bees have enough honey for winter? European bees store honey and eat off it all winter long. They cluster together for warmth and move from frame to frame, eating their fill and surviving. Compared to the bare six weeks that comprises the life of a summertime bee, in winter the sisters live up to six months.

The winter rages on and as long as they have food, they will not feel its blast. But what if I stole too much honey last fall? What if they get as close as February, or even March, and die off bare days before the first flowers of spring provide their nectar?

It can happen. It happened to me before. I feel so frustrated when I discover in April that a hive didn't quite make it. The bees are even less happy.

That's the real question. Do we have enough for the future? As Haggai put it, is there seed left in the barn?

At Christmastime we expend too much energy writing out cards, buying gifts, putting up decorations, making all the special treats, giving people all the special treats, accepting other special treats from folks, and eating all those other special treats, then driving or flying and feasting and hosting and visiting.

Have we any seed left in the barn? Do we have any reserves for the period after Christmas? Do we ever feel the Christmas spirit at any time during the season with all the things we have to do?

And we have to do these things. I'm not a Scrooge. But I think our approach to Christmas is wrong. Christmas is a marathon, and even if we pare down our expectations, it is still a time in which we are meant to feel more keenly the ties that bind.

Seasons don't begin and end in a single day. There is no mad rush in autumn to do all the leaf raking and storm windowing. We don't brace for a single day of winter, hurriedly plant during a frenzied day of spring, or cram three months' worth of living into a solitary day of summer.

At least I don't.

If a summer picnic is rained out, we know we can plan for another weekend. The first leaves of autumn are only the beginning. One snowfall does not a winter make.

Seasons don't come and go in a day, but that's the way we treat Christmas. For most of us the holiday begins around sunset on Christmas Eve. Christmas is usually composed of one part worship service, three parts last-second shopping and wrapping, two parts frantic driving between one's relatives and five parts total collapse.

December 26 we put away the Christmas albums we never got around to enjoying, dump the tree in the burn pile, and sullenly wonder what happened to the holiday, while brooding over the ominous arrival of the new year.

51

Not a pretty sight, is it?

The church calendar knows nothing of this frenetic holiday. For Christendom, Christmas is a season that begins with the first Sunday of Advent and continues through the Feast of the Magi, known as Epiphany (January 6). Each week has a different focus for celebration and worship. In many countries gifts are given on December 6 or January 6, and many of the days in between. To cease singing Christmas carols on December 25 would strike many Christians around the world as ludicrous. Stop? We're just getting started.

Christmas is for the long haul. It's a season, not a day, and that requires some serious resolutions. Here are my Ten Commandments of Christmas:

1. Honor the Lord of the season — not through deprivation or some misplaced sense of solemnity. We have been waiting all year for the king's arrival. This is a holiday. Keep it holy by celebrating with friends and family.

2. Let your gift giving be joyful.

3. You shall not be a slave to the greeting cards.

4. You shall do one thing you have never done.

5. You shall destroy one sacred cow, ignore one holiday tradition, in order to give yourself more time. The babe will arrive whether you make your special fudge or not.

6. You shall play with the nativity set this Christmas.

7. Be resolved that December 26 is as much Christmas as the day before. (If nothing else, this allows you to take advantage of the sales. Did you ever think what great gifts you could give to people if they would only wait until December 27?)

8. Play a Christmas album loud enough to embarrass someone. (It doesn't matter which: Perry Como, the Chipmunks, or a concert choir.)

9. You shall visit one shut-in during the season and invite one lonely person into your home. Hospitality is part of the season. There was no room at the inn. Too often we have a mandatory guest list of people we have to entertain or visit. Tear it up. Pick something new to do this year.

10. Sometime around December 30, when the house is quiet except for the creaking of the boards and the distant chimes at

midnight, sing "O Come, All Ye Faithful," "O Little Town of Bethlehem," and "Silent Night" quietly to yourself. Worship the king.

Is there seed left in the barn? Is there any faith left for the day after Christmas?

The promise of Haggai is that God will bless with more than mere abundance. The vine, the fig tree, and the olive tree provided the staples of existence. Grapes for eating and wine for drink, figs to make a thick paste, and olives for oil and flavor. They had to be harvested in their season and pressed for preservation. Processed, they could be stored for months.

But pomegranates were luxuries. They're great fun to eat, but there's not tremendous nourishment. Most of the fruit is a woody pulp. Ah, but the sweetness of the seeds! They are more beautiful than diamonds, though almost as fragile as soap bubbles. Squeeze them and they burst. They will stain your clothes but good, too.

God not only plans for us to survive, he wants us to enjoy. God's gifts provide more than just nourishment. They provide pleasure. Look around you, God tells the people through Haggai. Do the vine, the fig tree, the pomegranate, and the olive tree still yield nothing? Nonsense. There is pleasure now and pleasure in the future. Count on it.

By leaving seed you were acknowledging God's gifts of the past harvest, even while you enjoy them in the present. By setting aside seed corn you were proclaiming you could count on God's goodness even as you expressed faith in the future. By leaving honey on the comb you were expressing your faith that spring will come again.

Which reminds me of another formulation of faith that mirrors our trust in God's nature, and that is our trust in the nature of God: *Christ has died, Christ is risen, Christ will come again.*

And as the Lord spoke through Haggai, "And I will bless you."

53

For I Have Chosen You!

The word of the LORD came a second time to Haggai on the twenty-fourth day of the month: Speak to Zerubbabel, governor of Judah, saying, I am about to shake the heavens and the earth, and to overthrow the throne of kingdoms; I am about to destroy the strength of the kingdoms of the nations, and overthrow the chariots and their riders; and the horses and their riders shall fall, every one by the sword of a comrade. On that day, says the LORD of hosts, I will take you, O Zerubbabel my servant, son of Shealtiel, says the LORD, and make you like a signet ring; for I have chosen you, says the LORD of hosts.
— Haggai 2:20-23

When I was a kid the night before Christmas was the longest night in the world.

There were only one or two clocks in our house as a general rule, and eventually eight of us kids. To forestall endless repetition of the question "What time is it?" our parents loaned us one of the clocks, and many times we'd sleep in only one or two rooms, waiting together.

Each in turn would wake, and quietly, so quietly, attempt to turn the luminescent dial towards ourselves, believing it possible that we would not rouse the others. All around us was darkness. Silence reigned. So did fear. We did not dare to stir from our room, for fear of frightening Santa Claus and breaking the charm of Christmas.

And each time the clock showed that absolutely no time had passed at all. The world had come to a dead stop halfway between dusk and dawn.

Prior to that night had been weeks of dreaming and hinting. Christmas was a sure thing. There were going to be presents. Even in difficult years our parents worked miracles. The only question was — what? What would our presents look like?

Finally the moment would come. The clock would become unstuck, the hands would swing down towards six, and our parents, bleary-eyed but game, would announce that we could see what Santa had brought us. Yes, what Paul had written was true: The night is far gone. The day is at hand.

The wonder of it all was magnificent, no question about it. The waiting would have been futile without the promise of Christmas as a reward.

But Christmas would not have been as sweet without the waiting. I'm convinced.

I knew even then that others opened their presents on Christmas Eve, but I could never understand that. Where was the fun WITHOUT that endless night of delicious waiting, knowing something good beyond measure lay beyond the dawn. I mean, you had your presents, you knew what they were, and THEN you went to sleep? Had the world gone crazy?

Had I been raised another way, of course, I'm sure I would have accepted it as normal. That's the trick, you know, understanding that everyone's background is different and delightful. Yes, you ate turkey for Christmas Day, but we had chili beans and tamales, and I wouldn't trade that for anything, and neither should you.

Once again, on the twenty-fourth day of the month, the Lord speaks through the prophet Haggai. Just like the last prophecy. Twice in one day! Probably no one was more surprised than Haggai.

Speak to Zerubbabel, governor of Judah, saying, I am about to shake the heavens and the earth, and to overthrow the throne of kingdoms; I am about o destroy the strength of the kingdoms of the nations, and overthrow the chariots and their riders; and the horses and their riders shall fall, every one by the sword of a comrade.
— Haggai 2:21-22

56

So audacious is this prophecy that there must have been some who laughed at its impossibility. Zerubbabel was no king. He was a governor of a tiny region on the edge of a province in a huge empire. He probably had no standing army, only a ceremonial guard.

Zerubbabel himself might have been nervous about all this, looking this way and that, hoping no one heard. If word of this were to get back to Darius, things could get a little sticky. The penalty for treason is final.

And others thought of personal and political glory. The whole world was going to pay. Shake the heavens and the earth, overthrow the throne of kingdoms. Chariots and warhorses were high tech. Armies fled in disarray at the sight of these magnificent war machines.

But no human general was going to lead this army. The key phrase that the riders would fall, "everyone by the sword of the comrade," makes it clear that this is God's victory. Just as Gideon sent most of his army packing so it would be clear this was God's victory and not Gideon's, just as it was the angel and not the Israelites who killed 185,000 Assyrians in a single night, just as Paul wrote that God's strength is revealed in our weakness, so too the final victory of peace over chaos will be the work of God and not ours.

Those who waited for a king like David didn't understand what God was talking about. And they'd forgotten how flawed a David could be. The sheer weight of this victory required that someone outside the human realm accomplish what appeared to be an impossible task. That task seems no less impossible today, considering the difficulties of the world's problems.

The thought of God's kingdom bursting in on creation, of God's will being done on earth as it is in heaven, is better than any Christmas. Indeed, the first real Christmas, as glorious as it is, remains only a foretaste of the victory of God, when Jesus shall come in triumph.

Thoughts of the ending go hand in hand with meditations on the begining. It's only natural that the prophecies of Jesus about the endtime are usually read as part of the lectionary in churches the week prior to and also the first weeks of Advent.

But when?

When will it happen? How long will we wait? The night inches along, history seems to have stopped, and we know the gift of God will be overwhelming, but the fact remains that it is not here yet.

For some the most important thing is to be able to predict how long this night will last, down to the day! It is not enough to say "soon." They want to be able to set their clock.

Haggai's words, elaborated by Zechariah, Malachi, and the prophet who retold Daniel's story, make it clear God will set it all right. But other than the fact that "I am about to destroy the strength of the kingdoms," no clear timetable is set.

For some these verses are part of a great code that requires obscure interpretations to fit them into a scheme that reveals the exact dates and sequences of endtime events.

During my life the date for the end has been set many times. Throughout the early seventies books were printed that explained why the end had finally come. The years slipped by. And there was the time in 1987 that I received an almost incomprehensible book called *88 Reasons Why the Rapture Could Be in 1988*. Believe it or not, a sequel appeared a year later explaining why the author was only slightly off.

There is a growing realization, however, that a calendar interpretation of the apocalyptic literature is neither consistent with the intent of scripture, nor in the least bit useful.

The real message of these passages, written to those of us who live in tough times, is HOLD ON! Please. Hold on just a little longer. The night is far gone. The day is at hand. You can make it.

In the meantime, we have to remain alert. Students cram for tests because they know when the end of the term is approaching. They could have studied steadily all semester and been ready at any time to take the exam.

Because we don't know the end of God's term, we have to be ready for the test always.

Jesus warned his apostles in strong language: "Beware that no one leads you astray. Many will come in my name and say, 'I am he!' and they will lead many astray. When you hear of wars and rumors of wars, do not be alarmed; this must take place, but the end is still to come. For nation will rise against nation, and kingdom against kingdom; there will be earthquakes in various places; there will be famines. This is but the beginning of the birthpangs" (Mark 13:5-8).

One thing is certain: "But about that day or hour no one knows, neither the angels in heaven, nor the Son, but only the Father" (Mark 13:32). This is a literal statement that many literalists ignore!

If Haggai expected God's kingdom to happen in his lifetime, then he was wrong. But no more wrong than Jesus, who said one of the most puzzling things in the scriptures: "Truly I tell you, this generation will not pass away until all these things have taken place" (Mark 13:30).

C. S. Lewis once wrote that this statement of Jesus must be correct because no one would have put these words into his mouth when on the surface it looks as if Jesus was wrong.

But as Lewis also pointed out, this statement proved that God did not cheat when it came to the incarnation. While fully God and in control of the universe, he was also fully human and shared our frailties.

I think the real problem is that none of us really understands the nature of divine time. We speak of eternity, but assume that heaven runs on Eastern Standard Time. It's true. There's an unspoken assumption that God and the redeemed of the Lord are watching the earth.

God is not bounded by linear time. Eternity probably contains all moments. All time is accessible from that one point.

I liken God's perspective to a film reel. If we hold the reel in our hand we can turn to any frame and see what is happening. Moreover, in our view the die is cast. We know what has and will take place.

But the people in the movie still have free will. They will travel from one film cell to another, making choices, and bound to touch all the bases before coming home.

In like fashion we travel from one second to the next. As Shakespeare wrote in his sixtieth sonnet:

Like as the waves make towards the pebbled shore,
So do our minutes hasten to their end;
Each changing place with that which goes before ...

Or even better, as Macbeth, in the play of that title, says:

Tomorrow, and tomorrow, and tomorrow
Creeps in this petty pace from day to day
To the last syllable of recorded time,
And all our yesterdays have lighted fools
The way to dusty death.

We are prisoners of linear time. Although space and time are part of the same fabric in our universe, we cannot travel freely in time as we can in space. We live each moment in succession, remember as best we are able what occurred in the past, while pressing forward into the future at the rate of sixty seconds every minute and sixty minutes every hour.

Our mistake is to insist that God experiences time in the same fashion.

My favorite illustration of how God's time differs from ours is contained in the twelfth chapter of Revelation. Just as Haggai, in 2:21, looks ahead to when God will shake the heavens and the earth, so this final book of the Bible describes in even greater detail what may be expected. But it does this with images that are not intended to be translated into chronological sequences.

The twelfth chapter of Revelation introduces the woman clothed with the sun, who seems to be a combination of Mary, the nation of Israel, and the church. She is in great labor, and about to give birth to the child who will rule all the nations, reminiscent of the prophecy in Haggai. But the great red dragon, who we are told later is called both the Devil and Satan (Revelation 12:9), waits to devour her child even as he is about to be born.

However, in what seems to be a re-enactment of the death and resurrection of Jesus, the child, upon being born, is carried up to the throne of God, while the woman, who may now represent the early Christian church which abandoned Jerusalem before its destruction, flees to the desert.

"Now war arose in heaven," reads Revelation 12:7. Michael is on one side and the dragon is on the earth, and the dragon "was thrown down to the earth, and his angels were thrown down with him" (Revelation 12:9).

Is something wrong here? The timing of the events seems askew. Satan and his angels are thrown out of heaven after the birth of Jesus in this story. When DID the fall of Lucifer occur? Was it in ages past, before the dawn of time on earth? These passages ...

> *How you are fallen from heaven, O Day Star, son of Dawn!*
> *How you are cut down to the ground, you who laid the*
> *nations low! You said in your heart, "I will ascend to*
> *heaven; I will raise my throne above the stars of God; I*
> *will sit on the mount of assembly on the heights of Zaphon;*
> *I will ascend to the tops of the clouds, I will make myself*
> *like the Most High."*   — Isaiah 14:12-14

and:

> *Moreover the word of the LORD came to me: Mortal,*
> *raise a lamentation over the king of Tyre, and say to him,*
> *Thus says the Lord GOD: You were the signet of perfec-*
> *tion, full of wisdom and perfect in beauty. You were in*
> *Eden, the garden of God; every precious stone was your*
> *covering, carnelian, chrysolite, and moonstone, beryl,*
> *onyx, and jasper, sapphire, turquoise, and emerald; and*
> *worked in gold were your settings and your engravings.*
> *On the day that you were created they were prepared.*
>
> *With an anointed cherub as guardian I placed you;*
> *you were on the holy mountain of God; you walked among*
> *the stones of fire. You were blameless in your ways from*
> *the day that you were created, until iniquity was found in*
> *you. In the abundance of your trade you were filled with*
> *violence, and you sinned; so I cast you as a profane thing*
> *from the mountain of God, and the guardian cherub drove*
> *you out from among the stones of fire. Your heart was*
> *proud because of your beauty; you corrupted your wisdom*

*for the sake of your splendor. I cast you to the ground; I
exposed you before kings, to feast their eyes on you.*
— Ezekiel 28:11-17

... are thought by some to include, as a secondary meaning at
the very least, descriptions of the fall of the brightest of angels in
the dim and distant past.

And Jesus himself said, "I saw Satan fall like lightning from
heaven" (Luke 10:19). This was in the middle of his ministry. Yet
John quotes Jesus, not long before the crucifixion, as saying, "Now
is the judgment of the world, now shall the ruler of this world be
cast out...." That's towards the end of the ministry.

The question of when Satan was cast from heaven is meaningless in chronological terms. If it happened in eternity the event can
be described from the perspective of the past, the present, and the
future with equal accuracy.

Also meaningless is any question of when God's kingdom is
installed, and on what day we shall see the Lord return in glory.
When we ask if Haggai was wrong, when we whisper the question,
"Was Jesus wrong?" the answer is, of course, no. The events of
eternity will happen at their own pace, have already happened, will
happen, are happening.

Make no mistake. Christmas is coming. Big time.

In the meantime, what is to be our attitude? How are we to live
this long Advent?

For one thing, we are to remember God's promise to make
Zerubbabel "like a signet ring." In the days before ballpoint pens,
signatures were often affixed in hot wax with one-of-a-kind signets.
These emblems would be rolled in the wax, leaving behind the
official mark of the king or another high official. Whether worn
on the hand as a ring, or around the neck on a string, these were as
important as credit cards in establishing identity.

We are God's signet ring. We are the proof of his presence on
earth. We are not God. We are not worthy. Yet God wants us to to
be the image of his presence through our ministries. In this way
people will know that God has set his seal of approval upon the
good works done in his name.

"I will take you," said God to Zerubbabel, and by extension, to us as well, "for I have chosen you." The Hebrew word for "take" resembles the term used for the manner in which God took both Enoch and Elijah, bypassing death into LIFE. Just like the genie said to Aladdin in the Disney movie, "You ain't never had a friend like me!"

As David wrote in the twenty-third psalm, "Surely goodness and mercy shall follow me all the days of my life!" And to help sustain us during times of trouble, during those long nights of waiting, he also wrote, "He leadeth me beside the still waters."

Professor Graydon Snyder of the Chicago Theological Seminary used a striking illustration during the sermon he preached at my installation service at the Elkhart Valley Church of the Brethren. He reminded us that still waters are stagnant waters, polluted waters, difficult waters. God is the shepherd who leads us by these waters, which are not fit to drink, and takes us to greener pastures and swiftly moving streams. There are many times in our lives when we find ourselves by stagnant waters, yet the promise made by Haggai to Zerubbabel is as true for us. God will win our victories for us.

The ultimate apocalyptic imperative is the same advice we might give to someone who is in danger of freezing to death: "Stay awake and keep moving!" The people in Haggai's time were suffering from a deep spiritual malaise. They had been full of a dream to rebuild God's kingdom on earth, yet eighteen years went by and they hadn't built the Temple. This funk was affecting everything, from the economy to the climate and the crops.

Haggai told the people to get up and do something. Build the temple. See what happens. We do not believe we are saved by works. Yet there's no question that it's hard for us to believe while lying on our backs and moping. We are God's people, wearing God's mark for all the world to see. Get up and do something to build his kingdom. His grace saves you, not your works, but it is surprising how works can help you say, "I believe," by making you look beyond yourself to something greater. You can see the communion of saints when you work among them. You can live in

God's kingdom by building. And you will know, by extension, the dreamer when you share the dream.

I wonder what Haggai thought, after receiving two prophecies in one day. Did he wonder if this were only the beginning, if God might start talking through him three, four, five times a day? Like the rookie who hits a couple of singles or a home run in his first game. Does Haggai imagine this will happen again and again and again?

Some only get one trip to the major leagues. That's not bad. Most of us don't get a shot at all. Regardless of what Haggai thought, this was his high-water mark. There are no more recorded prophecies attached to his name. Was he disappointed? Did he look back to that golden age, so very short, and say to his grandchildren, "You should have seen me when"?

Or maybe he realized that the arrival of God's spirit is a gift. We too may be infused with holy joy for a moment or an hour. We can't repeat the sensation on cue and we shouldn't try. Like bolts of lightning or gentle breezes, God moves among his people, making his presence felt or known. Success as the world judges is no standard by which to mark our faithfulness. God may speak through us once or throughout a lifetime. Rest assured it has nothing to do with our own worthiness. Nor should it be a cause for resentment when God chooses others to be his instruments.

Haggai was called to serve God as prophet for a short time, but he was called to be a disciple all the days of his life. So are we. Whether we are shepherds, drawn to the manger by the singing of angels, or magi called by the sign of a star, our task is the same, to draw attention not to ourselves, but to the king, now an infant lying in a manger, but soon and very soon, the glorious king and redeemer of the world.

So come all ye faithful, joyful and triumphant. Join Haggai at the foundation of the temple. Sweat a little. Sing a little. Keep your feet on the ground. Set and accomplish the small goals.

You're building the kingdom. The real kingdom. The eternal kingdom. A brick at a time.

So the elders of the Jews built and prospered, through the prophesying of the prophet Haggai and Zechariah son of Iddo. They finished their building by command of the God of Israel and by decree of Cyrus, Darius, and King Artaxerxes of Persia; and this house was finished on the third day of the month of Adar, in the sixth year of the reign of King Darius. The people of Israel, the priests and the Levites, and the rest of the returned exiles, celebrated the dedication of this house of God with joy.

— Ezra 6:14-16